W9-CKR-012

Cheese
Balls

40 celebratory and cheese-licious recipes

Cheese Balls

DENA RAYESS

photographs by
Heami Lee

CHRONICLE BOOKS
SAN FRANCISCO

Library of Congress Cataloging-in-Publication Data:
Names: Rayess, Dena, author.
Title: Cheese balls / Dena Rayess.
Description: San Francisco : Chronicle Books, [2018] | Includes index.
Identifiers: LCCN 2017061271 | ISBN 9781452171364 (hardcover : alk. paper)
Subjects: LCSH: Cooking (Cheese) | LCGFT: Cookbooks.
Classification: LCC TX759.5.C48 R39 2018 | DDC 641.6/73—dc23 LC record available at https://lccn.loc.gov/2017061271

Manufactured in China

Design by **VANESSA DINA**
Photographs by **HEAMI LEE**
Food styling by **VICTORIA GRANOF**
Prop styling by **ASTRID CHASTKA**
Typsetting by **HOWIE SEVERSON**

10 9 8 7 6 5 4 3 2 1

Chronicle books and gifts are available at special quantity discounts to corporations, professional associations, literacy programs, and other organizations. For details and discount information, please contact our corporate/premiums department at corporatesales@chroniclebooks.com or at 1-800-759-0190.

Chronicle Books LLC
680 Second Street
San Francisco, California 94107
www.chroniclebooks.com

INTRODUCTION

There's nothing quite like a cheese ball. No other food can gather people so quickly around the table or induce bigger smiles. Not just limited to holiday get-togethers, this little book of cheese in the round will guide and inspire you to live that cheese ball lifestyle all year long. From family-friendly balls to please a variety of tastes to lazy weekend luxuries, from fresh, light balls that give a break from the decadence to seasonal balls that get fancy, each no-fuss recipe is just the right amount of indulgent.

For most of the recipes, unless noted otherwise, it is easier to combine the dairy ingredients if they sit at room temperature for about 30 minutes or so to soften up. In addition, the stand mixer (or any sort of blending kitchen appliance, such as a handheld mixer or food processor) makes these straightforward recipes even easier to pull off. However, if you find yourself in a situation where your guests text that they're five minutes away, you still haven't hidden all your messy things, and you may or may not be wearing pants, don't overthink it—just use your hands.

Happy cheese balling!

Cheese-Scaping

THE BASIC BALL

Here's how to shape a basic cheese ball so you get that perfectly round shape. It's easier than you think.

1. Spoon the cheese mixture onto the center of a large piece of plastic wrap.

2. Gather the ends of the plastic and twist to close, forming a ball with the cheese mixture. Refrigerate for at least 30 minutes to set. (The cheese ball can be refrigerated overnight.)

HOW TO TOAST NUTS

Quite a few recipes in this book call for nuts, either in the cheese ball or to decorate the outside. Toasted nuts take your cheese ball to the next level.

1. Preheat the oven to 350°F [180°C]. Spread the nuts into a single layer on a rimmed baking sheet and bake until toasted and fragrant, 8 to 10 minutes. Set aside to cool.

Not all cheese balls, despite the name, must be round to be enjoyed. The following shaping and decorating ideas range from simple to more daring, involved projects. For the best results, all of these shapes should be made after making any of the cheese ball recipes in the following chapters, but before adding the toppings.

CHEESE WHEEL

This shape is perfect for cheese balls that feature a topping that is drizzled (like the Brie with Cranberries, page 82) or is paired with stackable ingredients (like the Queso, page 39).

1 cheese ball, without the topping

1. Remove the cheese ball from the fridge and remove the plastic wrap. Do not discard the plastic.

2. Using the palms of your hands, push down on the ball to create a flat top. The wheel should be about 3 to 4 in [7.5 to 10 cm] wide and 1½ in [4 cm] tall.

3. Rotate the cheese wheel and use the plastic wrap to smooth out the sides. Continue with the chosen recipe or re-cover in plastic and refrigerate if not immediately using.

CHEESE LOG

This classic shape is ideal for cheese balls that blur the lines between spread and ball, like Horchata (page 45) and Mushroom and Herb (page 90).

1 cheese ball, without the topping

1. Remove the cheese ball from the fridge and remove the plastic wrap. Discard the plastic.

2. Tear off a large piece of clean plastic wrap, place it on a work surface, and place the ball in the center. Drape half of the plastic wrap over the top of the cheese ball.

3. Using the palms of your hands, roll the cheese ball back and forth, slowly pushing the ball outward to form a log shape that's approximately 7 to 8 in [17 to 20 cm] long and 1½ in [4 cm] tall.

4. Gently press the ends until smooth. Continue with the chosen recipe or re-cover in plastic and refrigerate if not immediately using (simply reroll the bottom if it flattens).

MINI BALLS

These lend themselves to creating eye-catching presentations for parties: stack them on top of each other, distribute them randomly around your food spread, stick the suggested dipper or cracker into each ball. Try recipes that don't have complex mix-ins or toppings, like the Garden Herb (page 53), which will be easier to divide into mini balls.

1 cheese ball, without the topping
1 topping

1. Remove the cheese ball from the fridge and remove the plastic wrap. Discard the plastic.

2. Using an ice cream scoop, divide the cheese ball into small mounds, approximately 1 Tbsp each; you should get 12 to 15 mini balls from an 8-oz [230-g] cheese ball.

3. Using the palms of your hands, roll each mound into a smooth, even ball.

4. Continue with the chosen recipe or cover each mini ball in plastic and refrigerate if not immediately using. Roll each mini ball in the chosen topping just before serving.

OWL

The owl and hedgehog shapes are best with recipes that use nuts as the garnish, like the Classic (page 17), because they'll be easy to apply and have the biggest visual impact. For a more strik-ing presentation, I recommend doubling the recipe (both the topping and cheese ball) so that you can make a large owl.

1 cheese ball, without the topping
1 topping
3 small nuts (such as pistachios or peanuts)

1. Remove the cheese ball from the fridge and remove the plastic wrap. Discard the plastic.

2. To make the feet, using an ice cream scoop, scoop about 2 Tbsp from the cheese ball. Divide the mixture in half. Using the palms of your hands, roll each mound into a smooth, even ball and set aside.

3. To make the body and head, using the palms of your hands, roll the remaining cheese ball into a large, rounded oval. Place one end of the oval on a serving plate and gently press down to flatten the top. As you press down to create the head, the bottom should also flatten, which helps to create a stable base for the owl to stand on its own (it's best to work on the serving plate since it will be hard to move the owl once finished). With your fingers, pinch the top of the head to form two ears.

4. Smooth out the body and ears with your hands and place the feet at the base of the body.

5. To create the feathers, coat the back of the owl with three-quarters of the topping, starting

from the bottom and working your way up to the back of the head. Place a thin layer in between the ears.

6. To form the face, pat a little of the leftover topping on the side of the head, going in about ¼ in [6 mm]. To make the eyes, place 2 nuts about 1 in [2.5 cm] apart from each other in the middle of the face. To make the nose, cut the last nut in half crosswise and place one half of the nut, pointed-side facing down, slightly below the eyes. Discard the other half of the nut. Refrigerate if not using immediately.

HEDGEHOG

Whip up this beautifully kitschy shape for any retro-inspired shindig. Much like the Owl, the bigger the Hedgehog the better, so consider doubling the recipe.

1 cheese ball, without the topping

5 small nuts (such as pistachios or peanuts)

1½ to 2 cups [150 g to 200 g] sliced almonds or 1 topping

1. Remove the cheese ball from the fridge and remove the plastic wrap. Discard the plastic.

2. To make the body, using the palms of your hands, roll the cheese ball into a large, rounded oval. Place the oval, rounded-side down, on a plate and gently press down to flatten the bottom, which helps to create a stable base for the hedgehog to stand on its own (it's best to work on the serving plate since it will be hard to move the hedgehog once finished).

3. To form the snout, determine which end of the oval will be the front of the hedgehog. With your fingers, shape the front into a rounded triangle to form the snout, shaping the tip so that it points out and off of the plate.

4. To make the nose, cut a nut in half and place at the end of the snout. To make the eyes, place 2 nuts about 1 in [2.5 cm] from the nose tip, about a ½ in [1.25 cm] apart.

5. If using sliced almonds for the quills, starting at the end of the hedgehog, place the sliced almonds at an angle into the cheese, working in horizontal rows. Continue placing the almonds in rows until about 1 in [2.5 cm] above the eyes. If using a topping for the quills, press the topping onto the body of the hedgehog, starting from the end and working up the body until about 1 in [2.5 cm] above the eyes. Refrigerate if not using immediately.

PUMPKIN

This quick, under-five-minutes trick will transform any cheese ball into a pumpkin work of art. Complete the fall fantasy by using this shape for the Pumpkin Pie ball (page 79).

1 cheese ball, without the topping
Four 14-in [35.5-cm] pieces of kitchen twine
1 topping
1 bell pepper stem (for savory cheese balls) or 1 cinnamon stick (for sweet cheese balls)

1. Remove the cheese ball from the fridge, keeping it covered in plastic wrap.

2. On a flat surface, lay out a piece of kitchen twine. Lay another piece of twine perpendicular to the first, forming a cross. Place the remaining two pieces of twine across the upper-left and -right sections respectively, forming an X, so that there are eight spaces. Place the wrapped cheese ball in the center, where all the twine pieces intersect. Tie together the ends of each of the four pieces tightly on top of the cheese ball.

3. Press down on the very top, where the knots of twine intersect, with your index finger until the sections begin to expand out.

4. Gently cut away the twine and remove the plastic wrap. Smooth out any areas where the plastic wrap made impressions. Refrigerate if not using immediately. About 1 minute before serving, pat the outside of the pumpkin ball with the chosen topping and place the bell pepper stem or cinnamon stick on top.

13

Crowd-Pleasers

These classics are instant
family favorites that
even Grandma will enjoy.

Classic

Served alongside boozy martinis, this is the classic cheese ball of yesteryear. A few updates make it perfect for family get-togethers and retro-chic parties alike. This recipe sneaks in a small amount of Brie to add an extra layer of creamy goodness that will make guests proclaim, "This is the best cheese ball ever!"

8 oz [230 g] cream cheese, at room temperature

½ cup [65 g] shredded sharp cheddar cheese

2 oz [60 g] Brie cheese, rind removed

1 Tbsp Worcestershire sauce

¼ to ½ tsp hot sauce, or to taste

½ tsp garlic powder

½ tsp onion powder

¼ cup [10 g] chopped fresh flat-leaf parsley

6 oz [170 g] toasted pecans (see page 8 for How to Toast Nuts)

**Prep time
55 minutes**

1. Combine the cream cheese, cheddar, Brie, Worcestershire sauce, hot sauce, garlic powder, and onion powder in a bowl. With an electric mixer, beat on medium speed until incorporated. Add the parsley and continue to beat on low speed until just combined. Form the mixture into a ball and refrigerate until set (see page 8 for instructions).

2. While the cheese ball sets, coarsely chop the pecans and spread on a rimmed plate.

3. About 30 minutes before serving, remove the cheese ball from the fridge. Roll the ball in the pecans, pressing them firmly to the ball, until completely covered. Let soften at room temperature for 30 minutes. Serve.

Serve with: Ritz Crackers, crostini, assorted sliced raw vegetables (carrots, celery, radishes, green beans)

Spinach-Artichoke

Arguably the best dip at any party, the magical combination of spinach, artichoke, sour cream, and cheese only gets better in cheese ball form. These mini cheese balls are best served at room temperature, but they can also be warmed up on low heat in the oven for a couple of minutes.

3 Tbsp olive oil

3 garlic cloves, minced

½ cup [90 g] canned artichoke hearts, drained and coarsely chopped

½ cup [90 g] frozen spinach, thawed and squeezed of any water

⅓ cup [80 g] sour cream

⅓ cup [10 g] plus 1 Tbsp grated Parmesan

1 cup [140 g] fine dried bread crumbs

8 oz [230 g] cream cheese, at room temperature

Prep time
1 hour 30 minutes

1. In a medium skillet, heat 2 Tbsp of the olive oil over medium heat. Once hot, add the garlic and cook until fragrant but not browned, 30 to 60 seconds.

2. Add the artichoke hearts and spinach and cook until heated through and the spinach starts to wilt, 2 to 3 minutes.

3. Turn the heat to low, add the sour cream and 1 Tbsp of the Parmesan, and cook, stirring constantly, until heated through, 2 to 3 minutes. Remove from the heat and set aside to cool.

4. While the artichoke-spinach mixture cools, toast the bread crumbs. Heat the remaining 1 Tbsp olive oil in a medium skillet over medium heat, add the bread crumbs, and cook, stirring often, until just browned and fragrant, about 5 minutes. Remove from the heat, stir in the remaining ⅓ cup [10 g] Parmesan, and set aside to cool.

continued

5. Combine the cooled spinach-artichoke mixture and the cream cheese in a bowl. With an electric mixer, beat on medium speed until combined. Form the mixture into a ball and refrigerate until set (see page 8 for instructions). Once the cheese ball is set, continue with the instructions for shaping Mini Balls (see page 10), and then return to the fridge.

6. About 30 minutes before serving, remove the cheese balls from the fridge and let it soften at room temperature. Just before serving, spread the Parmesan bread crumbs onto a rimmed plate. Roll the balls in the bread crumbs, pressing them firmly to each ball, until completely covered. Serve.

Serve with: crostini, vegetable chips

Horseradish

This fragrant ball packs a punch thanks to two powerhouses of the stinky culinary arts: horseradish and blue cheese. I like toasted walnuts on the outside for a nice contrast in texture, but feel free to replace them with an herb like dill for an extra kick.

Nod to the classic combination of prime rib and horseradish sauce by pairing this cheese ball with an assortment of charcuterie, or if you're feeling extra fancy, mini prime rib sliders!

10 oz [285 g] cream cheese, at room temperature

2 Tbsp prepared horseradish

¼ cup [35 g] crumbled blue cheese

½ tsp Worcestershire sauce

Pinch of salt

Pinch of freshly ground black pepper

6 oz [170 g] toasted walnuts (see page 8 for How to Toast Nuts)

Prep time 40 minutes

1. Combine the cream cheese, horseradish, blue cheese, Worcestershire sauce, salt, and pepper in a bowl. With an electric mixer, beat on medium speed until incorporated. Form the mixture into a ball and refrigerate until set (see page 8 for instructions).

2. While the cheese ball sets, coarsely chop the walnuts and spread onto a rimmed plate.

3. About 30 minutes before serving, remove the cheese ball from the fridge. Roll the ball in the walnuts, pressing them firmly to the ball, until completely covered. Let soften at room temperature for 30 minutes. Serve.

Serve with: radishes, haricots verts, cocktail rye bread

Ranch and Bacon

This cheese ball is not for the faint of heart. If you want to make this vegetarian-friendly without skimping on the big flavor, replace the outer layer of bacon with something else that's salty and crispy, like lightly crushed store-bought fried onions.

12 oz [340 g] bacon, approximately 12 slices

8 oz [230 g] cream cheese, at room temperature

½ cup [65 g] shredded smoked Gouda cheese

3 Tbsp ranch dressing

⅓ cup [15 g] chopped fresh chives

**Prep time
1 hour**

1. Working in batches, cook the bacon in a large pan over medium heat, flipping occasionally, until crispy, 6 to 8 minutes. Transfer the bacon to a paper towel–lined plate and set aside to cool.

2. Combine the cream cheese, Gouda, and ranch in a bowl. With an electric mixer, beat on medium speed until incorporated. Add all but 2 Tbsp of the chives and beat on low speed until just combined. Form the mixture into a ball and refrigerate until set (see page 8 for instructions).

3. While the cheese ball sets, chop the cooled bacon into ¼-in [6-mm] pieces. Stir together the bacon and the reserved chives on a rimmed plate. (The bacon-chive mixture can be refrigerated in an airtight container for up to 3 days.)

4. About 30 minutes before serving, remove the cheese ball from the fridge. Roll the ball in the bacon-chive mixture, pressing the ingredients firmly to the ball, until completely covered. Let soften at room temperature for 30 minutes. Serve.

Serve with: sliced crudités like celery, radishes, and carrots; Ritz Crackers; onion jam; more bacon

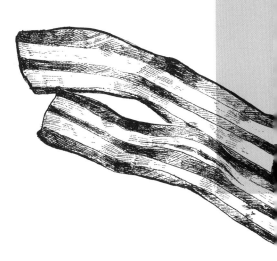

Apple Pie

There's nothing like an apple pie—it's instantly comforting and marks the beginning of fall, arguably the best season of the year. Using apple butter in this recipe creates a bold punch of sweet apple flavor, without the extra effort.

APPLE FILLING

1 sweet red apple, preferably Fuji or Gala

3 Tbsp butter

1 Tbsp water

1 Tbsp brown sugar

1 tsp ground cinnamon

½ tsp ground nutmeg

CHEESE BALL

12 oz [340 g] cream cheese, at room temperature

½ cup [140 g] apple butter

TOPPING

1 piecrust (thawed if frozen)

1½ tsp ground cinnamon

½ tsp ground nutmeg

**Prep time
35 to 45 minutes**

1. Make the apple filling: Peel the apple and dice into approximately ½-in [12-mm] pieces. Melt the butter in a medium pan over medium heat. Add the apple and cook, stirring occasionally, until soft and just beginning to brown, 10 to 12 minutes. Stir in the water, brown sugar, cinnamon, and nutmeg and cook until all ingredients are thoroughly incorporated and warmed through, 1 to 2 minutes longer. Remove from the heat and let cool.

2. Make the cheese ball: Combine the cream cheese and apple butter in a bowl. With an electric mixer, beat on medium speed until smooth. Add the cooled apple mixture and beat on low speed until just combined. Form the mixture into a ball and refrigerate overnight (see page 8 for instructions). This cheese ball needs a bit of extra time to set because it will most likely be quite soft at this stage.

continued

3. The next day, make the topping: Preheat the oven to 400°F [200°C]. Roll the piecrust onto a pie tin and sprinkle the cinnamon and nutmeg over it. Shake off the excess. Put the piecrust on a rimmed baking sheet and bake until browned, about 10 minutes. Set aside to cool.

4. Break the cooled piecrust into a fine crumble and into a bowl. For less mess, you can also crumble the piecrust inside its own tin, which you can then use to roll the cheese ball in!

5. About 10 minutes before serving (this ball tends to be softer, so keep it in the fridge until the last moment), remove the cheese ball from the fridge. Spread the piecrust onto a rimmed plate (if not using the tin). Roll the ball in the piecrust, pressing it firmly to the ball, until completely covered. Let soften at room temperature for 10 minutes. Serve.

Serve with: apple chips, butter waffle cookies

Cheesecake

This cheese ball is decadent. It's perfect for sitting out on the lanai with your favorite golden girls (and guys).

GRAHAM CRACKER CRUMBLE

Pulse 4 graham cracker sheets in a food processor until they're a fine powder. Combine the graham cracker powder with 2 Tbsp room temperature butter and 2 Tbsp brown sugar and smoosh the mixture with your fingertips until it resembles wet sand. Can be refrigerated in an airtight container for up to 3 days. Makes 1 cup [120 g].

1 lb [455 g] cream cheese, at room temperature

¼ tsp vanilla extract

⅔ cup [70 g] powdered sugar

1 cup [120 g] Graham Cracker Crumble (see left)

**Prep time
50 minutes**

1. Combine the cream cheese, vanilla, and sugar in a bowl. With an electric mixer, beat on medium speed until incorporated. Form the mixture into a ball and refrigerate until set (see page 8 for instructions).

2. About 10 minutes before serving (this ball tends to be softer, so keep it in the fridge until the last moment), remove the chilled cheese ball from the fridge. Spread the graham cracker crumble onto a rimmed plate. Roll the ball in the graham cracker crumble, pressing it firmly to the ball, until completely covered. Let soften at room temperature for 10 minutes. Serve.

Serve with: butter biscuits, apple slices, graham crackers, animal crackers

Port Wine

Make this purple ball the centerpiece for your next cheese plate. With its aged, jammy finish, this wine-centric offering pairs perfectly with a selection of hard cheeses, such as aged Gruyère, manchego, and Gouda, as well as stone fruit jams.

1 cup [140 g] raw sliced almonds

½ cup [100 g] sugar

1 cup [240 ml] Port

12 oz [340 g] cream cheese, at room temperature

4 oz [115 g] Brie cheese, rind removed

**Prep time
1 hour 10 minutes**

1. Preheat the oven to 350°F [180°C]. Line a rimmed baking sheet with parchment paper. Toss the almonds and sugar together in a bowl and spread into a single layer on the prepared baking sheet. Bake until caramelized and fragrant, 10 to 15 minutes. Set aside to cool.

2. In a small saucepan, bring the Port to a boil over medium-high heat, then turn the heat to low and simmer until reduced by half (½ cup/120 ml), 10 to 15 minutes. Remove from the heat and set aside to cool.

3. Combine 8 oz [225 g] of the cream cheese and the Brie in a bowl. With an electric mixer, beat on medium speed until smooth and combined. Cover the bowl in plastic wrap and set aside.

continued

4. Place the remaining 4 oz [115 g] cream cheese in a separate bowl. With the electric mixer running, add the cooled Port wine, 1 Tbsp at a time, and beat on medium speed until combined.

5. Uncover the bowl with the Brie–cream cheese mixture and add it to the Port–cream cheese mixture, gently mixing until just combined. Spoon the cheese mixture onto the center of a large piece of plastic wrap. Form the mixture into a ball and refrigerate until set (see page 8 for instructions).

6. While the cheese ball sets, coarsely chop the candied almonds and spread on a rimmed plate.

7. About 30 minutes before serving, remove the cheese ball from the fridge. Roll the ball in the almonds, pressing them firmly to the ball, until completely covered. Let soften at room temperature for 30 minutes. Serve.

Serve with: flatbread crackers, water crackers

Cookie Dough

Without even a touch of raw egg, anyone can dive into this ball of cookie dough without fear. This recipe is a perfect base for endless variations that can mimic your favorite cookies: swap the chocolate chips for chopped M&M's, sprinkles, or macadamia nuts, or stir in some cocoa powder or peanut butter.

1 cup [140 g] all-purpose flour

¾ cup [150 g] packed brown sugar

4 Tbsp butter, at room temperature

2 tsp vanilla extract

Pinch of salt

8 oz [230 g] cream cheese, at room temperature, cut into small pieces

⅔ cup [120 g] chocolate chips

⅔ cup [115 g] mini chocolate chips

Prep time
45 minutes

1. Combine the flour, brown sugar, butter, vanilla, and salt in a bowl. With an electric mixer, beat on medium speed until combined. With the mixer on, add the cream cheese, one piece at a time, and mix until smooth. With a spatula, stir in the chocolate chips until just combined. Form the mixture into a ball and refrigerate until set (see page 8 for instructions).

2. About 30 minutes before serving, remove the cheese ball from the fridge. Spread the mini chocolate chips onto a rimmed plate. Roll the ball in the chocolate chips, pressing them firmly to the ball, until completely covered. Let soften at room temperature for 30 minutes. Serve.

Serve with: spoons for scooping, butter biscuits, Nilla wafers, or (for the daring and/or obsessed) chocolate chip cookies

Afternoon Snacks

Sweet or savory, but always delicious,
these are an indulgent way to sit back, relax,
and enjoy something a little bit cheesy.

French Onion

This ball may have more steps and prep time than some others, but the reward is an indulgent, ultimate snack that is worth the extra effort. Try out different flavors of chips for the outer layer to create a new and unique spin on this recipe, from barbecue to SunChips to dill pickle.

2 to 3 Tbsp butter

1 yellow onion, sliced

8 oz [230 g] cream cheese, at room temperature

1 tsp garlic powder

1 Tbsp minced fresh chives

3 cups [60 g] plain potato chips

Prep time
1 hour 10 minutes

1. Melt the butter in a large pan over medium heat. Add the onion and cook, stirring occasionally, until deep brown and softened, 25 to 30 minutes. If the onion starts to burn, add up to 1 Tbsp of butter as needed and lower the heat—the goal is to get a nice caramelized flavor. Set aside to cool.

2. Once cool, coarsely chop the caramelized onion. Combine the onion, cream cheese, and garlic powder in a bowl. With an electric mixer, beat on medium speed until incorporated. With a spatula, stir in the chives until just combined. Form the mixture into a ball and refrigerate until set (see page 8 for instructions). Once the cheese ball is set, continue with the instructions for shaping the Cheese Log (see page 9), and then return to the fridge.

continued

3. While the cheese ball sets, put the potato chips into a resealable plastic bag and crush with your fingers or a rolling pin until broken into coarse crumbs.

4. Remove the cheese ball from the fridge 30 minutes before serving and let it soften at room temperature. Just before serving, spread the crushed potato chips onto a rimmed plate (make sure to add the chips at the last possible moment, so they don't get soggy). Roll the ball in the potato chips, pressing them firmly to the ball, until completely covered. Serve.

Serve with: ruffled or kettle-cooked potato chips, whole-grain chips, carrot slices

Buffalo Ball

This tangy ball is a fantastic crowd-pleaser for any game-day spread. To make the most of the potential toppings, shape this ball into a Cheese Wheel (see page 8).

12 oz [340 g] cream cheese, at room temperature

¼ cup [60 ml] plus 2 Tbsp store-bought buffalo wing sauce

2 Tbsp crumbled blue cheese

¼ cup [20 g] shredded mozzarella cheese

1 generous Tbsp minced fresh chives

TOPPINGS (OPTIONAL)

2 to 3 Tbsp shredded cooked chicken

2 to 3 Tbsp chopped cooked bacon

1 Tbsp minced fresh chives

Prep time
40 minutes

1. Combine the cream cheese, 2 Tbsp of the buffalo wing sauce, the blue cheese, and mozzarella in a bowl. With an electric mixer, beat on medium speed until incorporated. With a spatula, stir in the chives until just combined. Form the mixture into a ball and refrigerate until set (see page 8 for instructions). Once the cheese ball is set, continue with the instructions for shaping the Cheese Wheel (see page 8), and then return to the fridge.

2. About 30 minutes before serving, remove the cheese ball from the fridge and let it soften at room temperature. Just before serving, lightly brush the cheese wheel with the remaining ¼ cup [60 ml] buffalo wing sauce and arrange the toppings. You can pile on your chosen toppings any way you like, but I recommend arranging them in layers. Serve.

Serve with: sliced crunchy vegetables like celery, carrots, and radishes

Queso

You can have a lot of fun with this cheese ball. It's simple to make with shortcuts like using store-bought queso dip, and the types of delectable toppings to add on are just about endless.

12 oz [340 g] cream cheese, at room temperature

¼ cup [65 g] store-bought queso dip

1 or 2 jalapeños, roasted and chopped (see page 40)

¼ cup [40 g] crumbled queso fresco

2 Tbsp minced fresh cilantro

TOPPINGS

1 to 2 Tbsp cooked crumbled chorizo

2 to 3 Tbsp diced tomatoes

1 small jalapeño, thinly sliced

1 to 2 Tbsp crumbled queso fresco

1 Tbsp minced fresh cilantro

**Prep time
50 minutes**

1. Combine the cream cheese, queso dip, 1 or 2 jalapeños (depending on your desired heat level), and queso fresco in a bowl. With an electric mixer, beat on medium speed until fully combined. With a spatula, stir in the cilantro until incorporated. Form the mixture into a ball and refrigerate until set (see page 8 for instructions). Once the cheese ball is set, continue with the instructions for shaping the Cheese Wheel (see page 8), then return to the fridge.

2. Remove the cheese wheel from the fridge 30 minutes before serving and let it soften at room temperature. Just before serving, add the toppings. You can pile on your chosen toppings any way you like, but I recommend starting with a layer of chorizo, followed by the tomatoes, sliced jalapeño, and the queso fresco. Sprinkle cilantro over the top. Serve.

Serve with: tortilla chips, kettle-cooked chips

Jalapeño Popper

Spicy, cheesy, and with an outer layer of crispy goodness, this cheese ball takes on all the tasty components of a jalapeño popper and turns it into a delicious vessel for everyone to sink their chip into.

FOOTBALL SHAPE

It's easy to shape it into a football, if you follow the Hedgehog instructions (see page 12); just double the recipe, nix the snout, and arrange the toppings to mimic the football laces.

3 jalapeños

8 oz [230 g] cream cheese, at room temperature

½ cup [65 g] shredded pepper Jack cheese

5 Tbsp [75 ml] olive oil

½ cup [30 g] panko

Prep time
1 hour 10 minutes

1. Stick 2 of the jalapeños on skewers. Turn a gas burner to low and roast the jalapeños until charred on all sides, about 10 minutes. Once charred, immediately place the jalapeños in a sealable bowl and let steam for 5 to 10 minutes. Peel off and discard the skins and cut each jalapeño lengthwise. Scrape away the seeds and finely dice the jalapeño.

2. Combine the cream cheese and pepper Jack in a bowl. With an electric mixer, beat on medium speed until combined. With a spatula, stir in the roasted jalapeños to taste—use all of them if you prefer it spicy—until just combined. Form the mixture into a ball and refrigerate until set (see page 8 for instructions). Once the cheese ball is set, continue with the instructions for shaping a football (see left), and then return to the fridge.

continued

3. While the cheese ball sets, toast the panko. In a medium pan, heat 2 Tbsp of the olive oil over medium heat. Add the panko and toast, stirring often, until golden and crispy, 2 to 3 minutes. Set aside to cool.

4. Remove the cheese ball from the fridge 30 min-utes before serving and let it soften at room temperature.

5. While the cheese ball softens, make the fried jalapeño topping. Heat the remaining 3 Tbsp olive oil in a skillet over medium heat. Cut the remaining jalapeño into thin slices, discarding the seeds, and place in the hot oil. Fry until just begin-ning to brown at the edges, 2 to 3 minutes. Transfer the jalapeño slices to a paper towel–lined plate and set aside to cool.

6. Just before serving, spread the toasted panko on a rimmed plate (make sure to add the panko at the last possible moment, so it doesn't get soggy). Roll the ball in the panko, pressing it firmly to the ball, until completely covered. Top with the fried jalapeños and serve.

Serve with: tortilla chips, corn chips, warmed tortilla wedges

Herb and Jam

This is one of my go-to cheese balls because it is perfectly adaptable. Switch up the herbs and try out new and interesting jams for a surprising and low-effort snack. My favorite combinations are strawberry jam and rosemary, orange marmalade and thyme, or blackberry jam and mint.

12 oz [340 g] cream cheese, at room temperature

2 Tbsp jam or marmalade of your choice

2 to 3 Tbsp chopped fresh herb of your choice

5 oz [150 g] store-bought butter shortbread cookies (such as Walkers Shortbread fingers), approximately 8 cookies

**Prep time
1 hour 20 minutes**

1. Combine 4 oz [110 g] of the cream cheese and the jam in a bowl. With an electric mixer, beat on medium speed until incorporated. Form the mixture into a ball and refrigerate until set (see page 8 for instructions).

2. In a separate bowl, combine the remaining 8 oz [230 g] of cream cheese and 2 Tbsp of the herbs and beat with an electric mixer on medium speed until incorporated. If you're using a mild herb, such as thyme, add up to 1 Tbsp more of the herbs, if you like. Form the mixture into a ball and refrigerate until set (see page 8 for instructions).

continued

3. Remove the cheese ball from the fridge at least 1 hour before serving and let it soften at room temperature, so you can add the jam. Flatten the herb cheese ball into an 8-in [20-cm] disk. Center the jam cheese ball on top of the disk and, using the plastic wrap, draw up the sides of the herb cheese disk so that it completely envelops the jam cheese ball. Pinch the ends of the herb ball together to seal the jam ball inside. Re-cover the cheese ball in plastic and refrigerate for at least 30 minutes to set. (The cheese ball can be refrigerated overnight.)

4. While the cheese ball sets, pulse the cookies in a food processor until they're a fine powder. (Or put in a resealable plastic bag and crush repeatedly with a rolling pin.)

5. Remove the cheese ball from the fridge 30 minutes before serving and let it soften at room temperature. Just before serving, spread the shortbread crumbs onto a rimmed plate. Roll the ball in the shortbread crumbs, pressing them firmly to the ball, until completely covered. Serve.

Serve with: sea salt crackers, butter biscuits, shortbread cookies

Horchata

The beloved Mexican drink makes for a delicious, decadent dessert. After all, who doesn't love cinnamon and sugar? This ball makes a perfect no-fuss dessert for dinner parties or casual gatherings.

12 oz [340 g] cream cheese, at room temperature

3 Tbsp mascarpone

1 Tbsp vanilla extract

1 Tbsp brown sugar

3 Tbsp ground cinnamon

½ cup [100 g] granulated sugar

Prep time
40 minutes

1. Combine the cream cheese, mascarpone, vanilla, and brown sugar in a bowl. With an electric mixer, beat on medium speed until combined. Form the mixture into a ball and refrigerate until set (see page 8 for instructions).

2. While the cheese ball sets, stir together the cinnamon and sugar on a rimmed plate.

3. About 10 minutes before serving (this ball tends to be softer, so keep it in the fridge until the last moment), remove the chilled cheese ball from the fridge. Roll the ball in the cinnamon sugar, pressing it firmly to the ball, until completely covered. Let soften at room temperature for 10 minutes. Serve.

Serve with: sugar cookies, chocolate cookies, strawberries

Nutella

This famous cocoa-hazelnut spread blends perfectly into cheese ball form to create an indulgent treat for the end of the day (or even breakfast—no judgment). Think of this as an interpretation of your favorite crêpe. Go nuts and add bananas or strawberries, or dollop some whipped cream on top!

12 oz [340 g] cream cheese, at room temperature

⅓ cup [95 g] Nutella or other cocoa-hazelnut spread

¼ cup [30 to 40 g] finely chopped bananas, strawberries, or your fruit of choice (optional)

½ cup [70 g] salted roasted peanuts, coarsely chopped

**Prep time
50 minutes**

1. Combine the cream cheese and Nutella in a bowl. With an electric mixer, beat on medium speed until fully combined. With a spatula, stir in the fruit (if using) until just combined. Form the mixture into a ball and refrigerate until set (see page 8 for instructions).

2. Spread the chopped peanuts onto a rimmed plate.

3. About 10 minutes before serving (this ball tends to be softer, so keep it in the fridge until the last moment), remove the chilled cheese ball from the fridge. Roll the ball in the peanuts, pressing them firmly into the ball, until completely covered. Let soften at room temperature for 10 minutes. Serve.

Serve with: graham crackers, shortbread cookies

Baklava

Baklava is such a fantastic, underrated dessert, so of course it needs to be turned into a cheese ball!

A ROSE IS A ROSE

There will be lots of the deliciously fragrant rose water syrup left over, which can be used to drizzle on just about anything. My absolute favorite use of rose water syrup is in cocktails, especially a rose gimlet. To make one, combine 2 parts gin, 1 part fresh lime juice, and 1 part rose water syrup, and then shake with ice and strain into a coupe or cocktail glass. Garnish with a lime twist. Enjoy!

¼ cup [60 ml] water

½ cup [100 g] sugar

½ cup [120 ml] rose water

12 oz [340 g] cream cheese, at room temperature

¼ cup [60 g] goat cheese

1 cup [100 g] store-bought baklava, coarsely chopped

**Prep time
55 minutes**

1. In a small saucepan, bring the water, sugar, and rose water to a boil. Turn the heat to low and gently simmer for 7 to 10 minutes. Set aside to cool.

2. Combine the cream cheese, goat cheese, and ¼ cup [60 ml] rose water syrup in a bowl. With an electric mixer, beat on medium speed until combined. Taste and add more rose water syrup, 1 Tbsp at a time, if you like, and beat until combined. Form the mixture into a ball and refrigerate until set (see page 8 for instructions).

3. About 30 minutes before serving, remove the chilled cheese ball from the fridge. Spread the baklava onto a rimmed plate. Roll the ball in the baklava, pressing it firmly into the ball, until completely covered. Let soften at room temperature for 30 minutes. Serve.

Serve with: almond cookies, pecan cookies, sesame crackers

Fresh Flavors

Embrace the lighter side of
cheese balls with these
refreshing recipes fit
for any sun-soaked spread.

Garden Herb

Use bright, fresh, seasonal herbs for a beautiful and eye-catching contrast when guests dip into this ver-dant ball. For a fun visual twist, make these into mini cheese balls (see page 10) so partygoers can have a cheese ball of their very own!

12 oz [340 g] cream cheese, at room temperature

4 oz [115 g] Brie cheese, rind removed

¼ tsp garlic powder

2 Tbsp thyme leaves (from 10 to 15 sprigs)

¾ cup [25 g] chopped fresh flat-leaf parsley

1 Tbsp minced fresh rosemary

**Prep time
40 minutes**

1. Combine the cream cheese, Brie, garlic powder, and thyme in a bowl. With an electric mixer, beat on medium speed until incorporated. Form the mixture into a ball and refrig-erate until set (see page 8 for instructions).

2. While the cheese ball sets, stir together the parsley and rosemary on a rimmed plate.

3. About 30 minutes before serving, remove the chilled cheese ball from the fridge. Roll the ball in the herbs, pressing them firmly to the ball, until completely covered. Let soften at room tempera-ture for 30 minutes. Serve.

Serve with: crostini, sea salt crackers, herb-infused or plain honey

Greek Feta

This tangy cheese ball is a refreshing change from the heavier, more traditional balls of the past. If you want to give this cheese ball some crunch, pulse 10 to 15 pita chips in a food processor or blender and use them in place of the minced dill.

10 oz [285 g] cream cheese, at room temperature

⅔ cup [80 g] crumbled feta cheese

¼ cup [30 g] diced cucumber

2 to 3 Tbsp olive oil

½ cup [15 g] minced fresh dill

**Prep time
55 minutes**

1. Combine the cream cheese and feta in a bowl. With an electric mixer, beat on medium speed until incorporated. With a spatula, gently stir in the cucumber until just combined. Form the mixture into a ball and refrigerate until set (see page 8 for instructions).

2. About 30 minutes before serving, remove the chilled cheese ball from the fridge. Lightly brush the cheese ball with the olive oil. Spread the dill onto a rimmed plate. Roll the ball in the dill, pressing it firmly to the ball, until completely covered. Let soften at room temperature for 30 minutes. Serve.

Serve with: olive tapenade, lavash bread, pita chips, cucumber slices

Bruschetta

This cheese ball is a meal in and of itself. Packed with sun-dried tomatoes, fresh basil, and mozzarella and rolled in crunchy crostini, this ball puts a well-needed spin on a classic appetizer.

8 oz [230 g] cream cheese, at room temperature

1 cup [80 g] shredded mozzarella cheese

¼ cup [35 g] oil-packed sun-dried tomatoes, coarsely chopped

2 Tbsp minced fresh basil

2 to 3 Tbsp balsamic vinegar

10 store-bought crostini

**Prep time
50 minutes**

1. Combine the cream cheese, mozzarella, sun-dried tomatoes, basil, and balsamic vinegar in a bowl. With an electric mixer, beat on medium speed until combined. Form the mixture into a ball and refrigerate until set (see page 8 for instructions).

2. While the cheese ball sets, pulse the crostini in a food processor until they're the size of bread crumbs. Spread the crostini crumbs onto a rimmed plate. (The crostini crumbs can be stored in an airtight container at room temperature for up to 5 days.)

3. Remove the cheese ball from the fridge 30 minutes before serving and let it soften at room temperature. Just before serving, roll the ball in the crostini crumbs, pressing them firmly to the ball, until completely covered. Serve.

Serve with: crostini, water crackers, flatbread crackers, herb crackers

Muffuletta

This cheese ball mixes together fatty, aged meats and salty, pickled ingredients to create a savory indulgent snack that's perfect to take along on picnics, or to add to a charcuterie and cheese plate.

12 oz [340 g] cream cheese, at room temperature

¼ cup [30 g] shredded provolone cheese

1 tsp Dijon mustard

2 Tbsp store-bought olive tapenade

1 tsp minced pickled hot pepper (optional)

1½ oz [45 g] prosciutto

1½ oz [45 g] salami

1 Tbsp olive oil

1 cup [140 g] fine dried bread crumbs

**Prep time
45 minutes**

1. Combine the cream cheese, provolone, mustard, tapenade, and pickled hot pepper (if using) in a bowl. With an electric mixer, beat on medium speed until combined.

2. Coarsely chop the prosciutto and salami and add to the cheese mixture. With a spatula, stir together until just combined. Form the mixture into a ball and refrigerate until set (see page 8 for instructions). Once the cheese ball is set, continue with the instructions for shaping a Cheese Wheel (see page 8), and then shape the wheel into a rectangle about 2 to 3 in [5 to 7.5 cm] wide and 5 to 6 in [12.5 to 17.5 cm] long. Then return to the fridge.

continued

3. While the cheese ball sets, toast the bread crumbs. Heat the olive oil in a medium skillet over medium heat, add the bread crumbs, and cook, stirring constantly, until just browned and fragrant, 2 to 3 minutes. Set aside to cool. (The toasted bread crumbs can be stored in an airtight container for up to 3 days.)

4. Remove the cheese ball from the fridge 30 minutes before serving and let it soften at room temperature. Just before serving, spread the cooled bread crumbs onto a rimmed plate. Roll the ball in the bread crumbs, pressing them firmly to the ball, until completely covered. Serve.

Serve with: crostini, water crackers

Balsamic and Fig

By using dried figs, you don't have to wait for the right season to enjoy this sweet and savory cheese ball. There are dozens of different types of balsamic vinegar out there, from fruit-infused to more savory offerings, so this cheese ball is always a unique tasting experience!

8 oz [230 g] cream cheese, at room temperature

⅓ cup [35 g] shredded Gruyère

½ cup [90 g] chopped dried figs

1 Tbsp honey

½ cup [60 g] raw walnuts

2 Tbsp balsamic vinegar

1 or 2 fresh figs

**Prep time
50 minutes**

1. Combine the cream cheese, Gruyère, dried figs, and honey in a bowl. With an electric mixer, beat on medium speed until combined. Form the mixture into a ball and refrigerate until set (see page 8 for instructions).

2. While the cheese ball sets, put the walnuts in a spice blender or food processor and pulse into a fine meal (grind the walnuts in batches for the best results). Spread the walnut meal onto a rimmed plate. (The walnut meal can be stored in an airtight container for up to 1 week.)

continued

3. About 10 minutes before serving (this ball tends to be softer, so keep it in the fridge until the last moment), remove the chilled cheese ball from the fridge. Lightly brush the cheese ball with the balsamic vinegar and roll it in the walnut meal, pressing it firmly to the ball, until completely covered. Thinly slice 1 or 2 fresh figs and drape them over the top or side of the ball. Let soften at room temperature for 10 minutes. Serve.

Serve with: whole-wheat crackers, water crackers, flatbread crackers

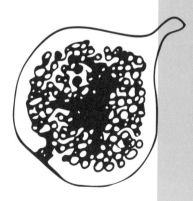

Goat Cheese and Honey

This is one of those balls that is minimal in effort but will have a huge impact. There is also a lot of room for adaptations. You can even use an infused honey, such as lavender or rosemary, for the inside filling and to drizzle over the ball.

½ cup [170 g] plus 2 Tbsp honey

1 cup [120 g] raw walnuts

8 oz [230 g] cream cheese, at room temperature

½ cup [115 g] goat cheese

Prep time
1 hour

1. Preheat the oven to 350°F [180°C]. Line a rimmed baking sheet with parchment paper.

2. In a small saucepan, bring ½ cup [170 g] of the honey to a boil. Add the walnuts, stir to coat, turn the heat to low, and simmer gently for 5 minutes.

3. Using a slotted spoon, transfer the honey walnuts to the prepared baking sheet and spread into a single layer. Bake the walnuts until golden, 5 to 7 minutes. Set aside to cool.

4. Combine the cream cheese, goat cheese, and the remaining 2 Tbsp honey in a bowl. With an electric mixer, beat on medium speed until combined. Form the mixture into a ball and refrigerate until set (see page 8 for instructions).

continued

5. While the cheese ball sets, coarsely chop the cooled honey walnuts and spread onto a rimmed plate.

6. About 10 minutes before serving (this ball tends to be softer, so keep it in the fridge until the last moment), remove the chilled cheese ball from the fridge. Roll the ball in the honey walnuts, pressing them firmly to the ball, until completely covered. Let soften at room temperature for 10 minutes. Serve.

Serve with: apple chips, whole-wheat crackers, sliced apples and pears

Lemon-Citrus–Poppy Seed

Inspired by the classic, sweet, and zesty breakfast muffin, this is a refreshing cheese ball that is perfect for any brunch, breakfast, lunch—really anytime you're looking for a delicate, citrus-forward offering.

12 oz [340 g] cream cheese, at room temperature

1 Tbsp grated lemon zest

¼ cup [70 g] orange marmalade

¼ cup [60 g] goat cheese

½ cup [70 g] poppy seeds

**Prep time
40 minutes**

1. Combine the cream cheese, lemon zest, marmalade, and goat cheese in a bowl. With an electric mixer, beat on medium speed until combined. Form the mixture into a ball and refrigerate until set (see page 8 for instructions).

2. About 10 minutes before serving (this ball tends to be softer, so keep it in the fridge until the last moment), remove the chilled cheese ball from the fridge. Spread the poppy seeds onto a rimmed plate. Roll the ball in the poppy seeds, pressing them firmly to the ball, until completely covered. Let soften at room temperature for 10 minutes. Serve.

Serve with: butter biscuits, crackers with seeds, short-bread cookies

Trail Mix

Packed with healthy, energy-boosting ingredients, this cheese ball is a no-fuss nosh that can be premade and packed on camping trips, hikes, or simply the trek to the table. My favorite trail mix is equal parts almonds, pistachios, and cashews, mixed with golden raisins, dried cranberries, and dark chocolate.

12 oz [340 g] cream cheese, at room temperature

2 Tbsp honey

1 cup [approximately 140 g] dried fruit, finely chopped (such as cranberries, blueberries, raisins, apricots)

¼ cup [approximately 140 g] sweet mix-ins (such as chocolate chips, coconut flakes, Chex, or candied ginger)

1 cup [approximately 120 g] assorted nuts and/or seeds (such as pistachio, almonds, cashews, pepitas), toasted (see page 8 for How to Toast Nuts)

**Prep time
1 hour 10 minutes**

1. Combine the cream cheese and honey in a bowl. With an electric mixer, beat on medium speed until combined. With a spatula, stir in the dried fruit and sweet mix-ins until just combined. Form the mixture into a ball and refrigerate until set (see page 8 for instructions).

2. While the cheese ball sets, coarsely chop the nuts and spread onto a rimmed plate.

3. About 30 minutes before serving, remove the chilled cheese ball from the fridge. Roll the ball in the nuts, pressing them firmly to the ball, until completely covered. Let soften at room temperature for 30 minutes. Serve.

Serve with: whole-wheat crackers, fruit and nut crisps

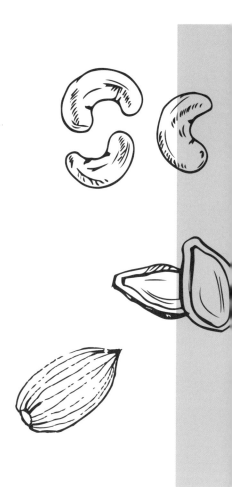

Holiday Statements

These cheese balls will be the perfect centerpiece to anyone's holiday gathering, sure to impress and start the season with a tasty bang!

Everything Bagel

This is the ultimate cheese ball for anyone who loves everything about everything bagels minus, well, the bagel. Covered in a magical combination of seeds and spices, I recommend doubling the topping, so you can sprinkle it on anything that needs an extra punch of salty goodness.

8 oz [230 grams] cream cheese, at room temperature

4 oz [115 g] Brie cheese, rind removed

4 oz [115 g] lox, coarsely chopped (optional)

EVERYTHING SPICE

2 Tbsp toasted white sesame seeds

2 Tbsp poppy seeds

2 Tbsp dried onion flakes

2 Tbsp dried garlic flakes

1 Tbsp black sesame seeds (optional)

½ tsp sea salt

**Prep time
40 minutes**

1. Combine the cream cheese and Brie in a bowl. With an electric mixer, beat on medium speed until combined. With a spatula, gently stir in the lox (if using) until incorporated. Form the mixture into a ball and refrigerate until set (see page 8 for instructions).

2. While the cheese ball sets, make the Everything Spice. Stir together all the ingredients in a shallow bowl and set aside.

3. About 30 minutes before serving, remove the chilled cheese ball from the fridge. Roll the ball in the Everything Spice, pressing it firmly to the ball, until completely covered. Let soften at room temperature for 30 minutes. Serve.

Serve with: cocktail rye bread, pretzel chips, pita chips, sliced lox

Holiday Ham

This meat-centric cheese ball is perfect for a casual Friendsgiving. Assuming you don't have leftover holiday ham lying around, go ahead and buy cooked ham (or turkey for a lighter variety) from the deli section. To mimic traditional holiday flavors, look for a ham with some sort of sweet glaze.

4 oz [115 g] diced ham, preferably maple or honey-glazed

10 oz [285 g] cream cheese, at room temperature

1 tsp whole-grain mustard

1½ tsp honey

Salt and freshly ground pepper

½ cup [25 g] minced fresh chives

**Prep time
40 minutes**

1. Combine the ham, cream cheese, mustard, and honey in a bowl. With an electric mixer, beat on medium speed until combined. Season with salt and pepper and stir to incorporate. Form the mixture into a ball and refrigerate until set (see page 8 for instructions).

2. About 30 minutes before serving, remove the chilled cheese ball from the fridge. Spread the chives onto a rimmed plate. Roll the ball in the chives, pressing them firmly to the ball, until completely covered. Let soften at room temperature for 30 minutes. Serve.

Serve with: sea salt crackers, water crackers, hot pepper–infused or plain honey, apple chips

Lasagna

Lasagnas, practically the best way to cook with cheese, tend to be an all-day cooking experience. This cheese ball gives everyone the beloved flavors of a classic holiday lasagna without eating away at your day.

8 oz [230 g] cream cheese, at room temperature

½ cup [40 g] shredded mozzarella

¼ cup [60 ml] tomato sauce

½ tsp garlic powder

2 Tbsp olive oil

½ cup [70 g] fine dried bread crumbs

2 Tbsp grated Parmesan

1 Tbsp minced fresh flat-leaf parsley

Prep time
40 minutes

1. Combine the cream cheese, mozzarella, tomato sauce, and garlic powder in a bowl. With an electric mixer, beat on medium speed until combined. Form the mixture into a ball and refrigerate until set (see page 8 for instructions).

2. While the cheese ball sets, toast the bread crumbs. Heat the olive oil in a skillet over medium heat, add the bread crumbs, and cook, stirring constantly, until just browned, 2 to 3 minutes. Remove from the heat, stir in the Parmesan and parsley, and set aside to cool. Spread the cooled bread crumb mixture onto a rimmed plate.

3. Remove the cheese ball from the fridge 30 minutes before serving and let it soften at room temperature. Just before serving, roll the ball in the bread crumbs, pressing them firmly to the ball, until completely covered. Serve.

Serve with: crostini, cheese crackers , whole-wheat crackers

Crab Cake

If possible, avoid the canned variety of crab and head over to the fish section of your local market to get the fresh stuff—the taste and consistency is worth the extra cost. Serve this as part of a beach-inspired late-afternoon spread as a treat to yourself. You deserve it.

12 oz [340 g] cream cheese, at room temperature

1 to 1½ tsp Old Bay Seasoning

1 tsp Worcestershire sauce

1 tsp Dijon mustard

Pinch of freshly ground pepper

½ cup [80 g] cooked fresh crabmeat (not canned)

1 Tbsp minced fresh flat-leaf parsley

2 Tbsp olive oil

1 cup [60 g] panko

**Prep time
45 minutes**

1. Combine the cream cheese, Old Bay, Worcestershire, mustard, and pepper in a bowl. With an electric mixer, beat on medium speed until combined. With a spatula, stir in the crabmeat and parsley until incorporated. Form the mixture into a ball and refrigerate until set (see page 8 for instructions).

2. While the cheese ball sets, toast the panko. In a medium pan over medium heat, heat the olive oil. Add the panko and toast, stirring often, until golden and crispy, 2 to 3 minutes. Set aside to cool.

3. Remove the cheese ball from the fridge 30 minutes before serving and let it soften at room temperature. Just before serving, spread the toasted panko on a rimmed plate. Roll the ball in the panko, pressing it firmly to the ball, until completely covered. Serve.

Serve with: saltines, water crackers, lemon wedges for squeezing, tartar sauce

Red, White, and Blue

Who says cheese balls need only be a cold-weather food? This fruit-centric ball would be a welcome addition to any summertime gathering, barbecue, or picnic. And with its patriotic colors, it's pretty darned perfect for post-fireworks snacking on the Fourth of July.

BLUEBERRY COMPOTE

½ cup [80 g] fresh blueberries

3 Tbsp granulated sugar

3 Tbsp water

CHEESE BALL

1 cup [175 g] fresh strawberries, sliced

1 Tbsp powdered sugar

12 oz [340 g] cream cheese, at room temperature

**Prep time
1 hour**

1. Make the blueberry compote: In a small pan, combine the blueberries, sugar, and water and bring to a boil. Turn the heat to low and simmer, stirring occasionally, until the mixture is thickened, about 10 minutes. Remove from the heat and set aside to cool; the compote will thicken as it cools. (The compote can be refrigerated in an airtight container for up to 3 days.)

2. Make the cheese ball: Gently stir together the strawberries and powdered sugar in a bowl until the strawberries are evenly coated in the sugar. Add the cream cheese, and with an electric mixer, beat on medium speed until just combined. Form the mixture into a ball and refrigerate until set (see page 8 for instructions). Once the cheese ball is set, continue with the instructions for shaping the Cheese Wheel (see page 8) and return to the fridge.

continued

3. About 30 minutes before serving, remove the blueberry compote from the fridge to let it come to room temperature.

4. Remove the cheese wheel from the fridge 10 minutes before serving and let it soften at room temperature (this ball tends to be softer, so keep it in the fridge until the last moment). Just before serving, spread the blueberry compote over the top of the wheel, letting some drizzle down the sides. Serve.

Serve with: butter biscuits, apple chips, apple slices, strawberries

Pumpkin Pie

This easy-as-pie treat is perfect for anyone craving their favorite Thanksgiving dessert. For a fun, seasonal presentation, shape this ball into a pumpkin.

DIY PUMPKIN

You can make your own pumpkin purée if you prefer. Simply remove the stem of a baking pumpkin, cut it in half, and scoop out the seeds. Place the pumpkin in a shallow baking pan, skin-side up, and add enough water so that it is about ½ in [12 mm] deep. Cover with aluminum foil and bake in a 350°F [180°C] oven until the inside is fork tender, 45 to 60 minutes. Scrape out the inside and process in a food processor until smooth.

12 oz [340 g] cream cheese, at room temperature

⅓ cup [75 g] pumpkin purée

1 Tbsp pumpkin spice

1½ Tbsp brown sugar, or to taste

1 piecrust (thawed if frozen)

**Prep time
1 hour**

1. Combine the cream cheese, pumpkin purée, pumpkin spice, and brown sugar in a bowl. With an electric mixer, beat on medium speed until combined. Form the mixture into a ball and refrigerate until set (see page 8 for instructions). Once the cheese ball is set, continue with the instructions for shaping the pumpkin (see page 13) and return to the fridge.

2. While the cheese ball sets, make the topping: Preheat the oven to 400°F [200°C]. Roll the piecrust onto a pie tin. Put the piecrust on a rimmed baking sheet and bake until browned, about 10 minutes. Set aside to cool.

continued

3. Break the cooled piecrust into a fine crumble and into a bowl. For less mess, you can also crumble the piecrust inside its own tin, which you can then use to roll the cheese ball in!

4. Remove the cheese ball from the fridge 30 minutes before serving and let it soften at room temperature. Just before serving, spread the piecrust onto a rimmed plate (if not using the pie tin). Roll the ball in the piecrust, pressing it firmly to the ball, until completely covered (or sprinkle on top if shaped into a pumpkin). Serve.

Serve with: cinnamon sugar cookies, Nilla wafers, waffle cookies

Brie with Cranberries

Topped with an incredibly easy-to-make cranberry sauce, this elegant cheese ball is an ideal addition to any New Year's Eve shindig or wintertime gathering.

CRANBERRY SAUCE

½ cup [100 g] sugar

¾ cup [170 g] frozen cranberries

2 Tbsp water

1 tsp grated orange zest

CHEESE BALL

8 oz [230 g] cream cheese, at room temperature

4 oz [115 g] Brie cheese, rind removed

1 tsp vanilla extract

Prep time
1 hour

1. Make the cranberry sauce: In a small saucepan, combine the sugar, cranberries, water, and orange zest and bring to a boil. Turn the heat to low and simmer, stirring occasionally, until the mixture is thickened and all the cranberries have burst, about 15 minutes. Remove from the heat and set aside to cool. (The cranberry sauce can be refrigerated in an airtight container for up to 1 week.)

2. Make the cheese ball: Combine the cream cheese, Brie, and vanilla in a bowl. With an electric mixer, beat on medium speed until combined. Form the mixture into a ball and refrigerate until set (see page 8 for instructions). Once the cheese ball is set, continue with the instructions for shaping the Cheese Log (see page 9) and return to the fridge.

continued

3. Remove the cheese ball from the fridge 10 minutes before serving and let it soften at room temperature (this ball tends to be softer, so keep it in the fridge until the last moment). Just before serving, spread the cranberry sauce over the top of the wheel, letting some drizzle down the sides. Serve.

Serve with: water crackers, toasted wheat crackers, apple slices

S'mores

No need to build a campfire for this beloved gooey childhood treat. Using marshmallow crème lessens the messy part of making and enjoying s'mores, although it's perfectly acceptable to lick your fingers when assembling this ball—it's that good. To really take this ball over the top, take a couple of mini marshmallows, stick them on a skewer, and toast them on a stovetop until they are darkened and bubbly. Artfully place the toasted marshmallows on the top and around the cheese ball.

6 oz [170 g] semisweet chocolate, coarsely chopped

10 oz [285 g] cream cheese, at room temperature

⅓ cup [80 g] marshmallow crème

1 cup [120 g] Graham Cracker Crumble (page 27)

**Prep time
50 minutes**

1. Separate out 2 oz [55 g] and set aside. Place 4 oz of chocolate in a microwave-safe bowl. Microwave, stirring every 30 seconds to avoid burning, until melted. Combine the melted chocolate and cream cheese in a separate bowl. With an electric mixer, beat on medium speed until incorporated.

2. Add the marshmallow crème and remaining chopped chocolate and continue to mix on low speed until just combined. Form the mixture into a ball and refrigerate until set (see page 8 for instructions).

3. Remove the cheese ball from the fridge 30 minutes before serving and let it soften at room temperature. Roll the ball in the Graham Cracker Crumble on a rimmed plate, pressing it firmly to the ball, until completely covered. Serve.

Serve with: graham crackers, gingersnap cookies, sliced strawberries

Evening Affairs

Use these innovative recipes
to up your game and make
unforgettable cheese balls.

Roasted Garlic

Have breath mints at the ready for this perfectly pungent cheese ball. With a smooth and creamy interior and a crunchy exterior, this cheese ball is a lovely addition to an Italian-inspired cheese plate or dinner.

2 garlic heads

4 to 6 Tbsp [60 to 90 ml] olive oil

10 oz [285 g] cream cheese, at room temperature

¼ cup [20 g] shredded mozzarella

½ cup [70 g] fine dried bread crumbs

2 Tbsp minced fresh flat-leaf parsley

**Prep time
1 hour 20 minutes**

1. Preheat the oven to 400°F [200°C].

2. Cut about ¼ in [6 mm] off the tops of the garlic heads. Gently peel away the papery skins of the bulbs until you are left with just a thin layer holding the cloves together.

3. Put the garlic heads onto a large sheet of aluminum foil and drizzle with up to 5 Tbsp [75 ml] of the olive oil, just enough to completely cover the garlic. Fold and seal the garlic in the foil packet. Bake until the cloves are browned and soft when poked with a thin knife or skewer, about 45 minutes. Set aside to cool.

4. Once cool to the touch, remove the cloves from the heads by pushing them out from the bottom. Mash the roasted garlic cloves with a fork until they're a coarse paste.

5. Combine the garlic paste, cream cheese, and mozzarella in a bowl. With an electric mixer, beat on medium speed until combined. Form the mixture into a ball and refrigerate until set (see page 8 for instructions).

6. While the cheese ball sets, toast the bread crumbs. Heat the remaining 1 Tbsp olive oil in a medium skillet over medium heat. Add the bread crumbs, stirring often, and cook until just browned, 2 to 3 minutes. Set aside to cool. Once cool, toss in the parsley.

7. Remove the cheese ball from the fridge 30 minutes before serving and let it soften at room temperature. Just before serving, spread the toasted bread crumbs onto a rimmed plate. Roll the ball in the bread crumbs, pressing them firmly to the ball, until completely covered. Serve.

Serve with: crostini, sea salt crackers, flatbread crackers, radish slices

Mushroom and Herb

This fungi-forward cheese ball is a sophisticated addition to any dinner party and pairs well with other umami-rich wintertime fare. Try shaping this into a log for an easily spreadable cheese ball (see page 9).

MUSHROOMS

2 Tbsp olive oil

½ cup [75 g] diced yellow onion

2 cups [160 g] sliced assorted mushrooms (such as cremini and shiitake)

2 garlic cloves, minced

1 Tbsp butter

¼ cup [60 ml] white wine

CHEESE BALL

12 oz [340 g] cream cheese, at room temperature

1 tsp minced fresh dill

1 tsp minced fresh thyme

10 store-bought crostini

**Prep time
1 hour**

1. Make the mushrooms: In a medium sauté pan, heat the olive oil over medium-high heat. Add the onion and cook until the edges start to brown, about 5 minutes. Add the mushrooms, garlic, and butter and cook until the liquid released from the mushrooms evaporates, about 5 minutes longer, stirring frequently.

2. Turn the heat to medium-low, add the wine, and cook until the wine is fully absorbed, about 2 minutes. Remove from the heat. Transfer the mushroom mixture to a food processor or blender and pulse until it resembles a coarse paste, or to your preferred consistency. Set aside to cool.

3. Make the cheese ball: Combine the cooled mushroom mixture, cream cheese, dill, and thyme in a bowl. With an electric mixer, beat on medium speed until incorporated. Form the mixture into a ball and refrigerate until set (see page 8 for instructions).

4. While the cheese ball sets, pulse the crostini in a food processor until they're the size of bread crumbs. Spread the crostini crumbs onto a rimmed plate. (The crostini crumbs can be stored in an airtight container at room temperature for up to 5 days.)

5. Remove the cheese ball from the fridge 30 minutes before serving and let it soften at room temperature. Just before serving, roll the ball in the crostini crumbs, pressing them firmly to the ball, until completely covered. Serve.

Serve with: water crackers, black pepper crackers, mini toasts

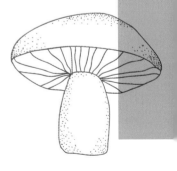

Lemon and Saffron

Saffron is such a unique flavor—it's almost indescribable. This cheese ball is perfect for saffron enthusiasts and newbies alike, thanks to its lemon pairing, which comes in the form of a crunchy, sweet outer layer. This recipe does involve a lot of lemon zesting, but the flavor that comes from it is so worth it. And when a recipe gives you lots of lemons to zest, make lemonade—literally—with the leftover lemons!

SAFFRON SYRUP

¼ cup [60 ml] water

¼ cup [85 g] honey

2 healthy pinches of saffron threads

CHEESE BALL

12 oz [340 g] cream cheese, at room temperature

¼ cup [60 g] goat cheese

¼ cup [20 g] grated lemon zest (from 2 or 3 lemons)

⅓ cup [65 g] turbinado sugar or light brown sugar

Prep time
1 hour 15 minutes

1. Make the saffron syrup: In a small saucepan, bring the water and honey to boil. Remove from the heat and immediately add the saffron. Let steep for 20 to 30 minutes. Strain the saffron syrup through a fine-mesh strainer and discard the saffron threads. Set aside. (The saffron syrup can be refrigerated for up to 1 week.)

2. Make the cheese ball: Combine the cream cheese and goat cheese in a bowl. With an electric mixer, beat on medium speed until combined. Add 4 to 5 Tbsp [60 to 75 ml] of the saffron syrup and beat until combined. Form the mixture into a ball and refrigerate until set (see page 8 for instructions).

continued

3. Remove the cheese ball from the fridge 10 minutes before serving and let it soften at room temperature (this ball tends to be softer, so keep it in the fridge until the last moment). Just before serving, stir together the lemon zest and sugar on a rimmed plate. Roll the ball in the lemon sugar, pressing it firmly to the ball, until completely covered. Drizzle the sugar-coated ball with the leftover saffron syrup and serve.

Serve with: shortbread cookies, almond cookies, sea salt crackers

Summertime Peach

There's nothing like an in-season peach, and better still, a peach that's grilled! This recipe can easily be adapted to whatever stone fruit is in season, from plums to apricots to nectarines. If stone fruit is not in season, go ahead and use canned peaches (just use a little less peach and add a tablespoon of the syrup it comes in).

1 Tbsp olive oil

¼ cup [90 g] sliced peach (from 1 small peach)

10 oz [285 g] cream cheese, at room temperature

¼ cup [60 g] mascarpone

¼ cup [50 g] sugar

2 Tbsp ground cinnamon

Prep time
50 minutes

1. In a grill pan, heat the olive oil over medium heat. Add the peach slices and grill until browned on each side, 6 to 7 minutes (skip this step if using canned peaches). Transfer the peaches to a plate and set aside to cool.

2. Once cool, finely chop the peach slices. Combine the chopped peach, cream cheese, and mascarpone in a bowl. With an electric mixer, beat on medium speed until combined. Form the mixture into a ball and refrigerate until set (see page 8 for instructions).

continued

3. Remove the cheese ball from the fridge 10 minutes before serving and let it soften at room temperature (this ball tends to be softer, so keep it in the fridge until the last moment). Just before serving, stir together the sugar and cinnamon on a rimmed plate. Roll the ball in the cinnamon sugar, pressing it firmly to the ball, until completely covered. Serve.

Serve with: apple, banana, or other fruit chips, hot pepper–infused or plain honey, Nilla wafers

Spicy Mango

If it's not there already, Chamoy sauce needs to be a part of your pantry now. Deliciously sweet, tangy, and spicy—all at the same time—this sauce can transform just about any tropical fruit into an addictive sweet and savory dessert. It can be found at any Mexican grocery store and some specialty supermarkets. Substitute hot pepper–infused honey if you can't find it.

12 oz [340 g] cream cheese, at room temperature

¼ cup [50 g] chopped mango, plus 2 slices for garnish (optional)

1 tsp grated lime zest

1 to 2 Tbsp Chamoy sauce

2 Tbsp sugar

1 Tbsp chili powder

**Prep time
40 minutes**

1. Combine the cream cheese, chopped mango, and lime zest in a bowl. With an electric mixer, beat on medium speed until combined. Drizzle in the Chamoy and gently stir with a spatula to swirl it together—you want ribbons of red to contrast with the orange mango mixture. Form the mixture into a ball and refrigerate until set (see page 8 for instructions).

continued

2. About 10 minutes before serving, remove the cheese ball from the fridge and let it soften at room temperature (this ball tends to be softer, so keep it in the fridge until the last moment). Just before serving, stir together the sugar and chili powder on a rimmed plate. Roll the ball in the sugar-chili mixture, pressing it firmly to the ball, until completely covered. Drape 2 mango slices over the top of the cheese ball, if using. Serve.

Serve with: sugar cookies, ginger cookies, apple chips

Rainbow

This is a cheese ball that you can have a lot of fun with. Treat this like a childhood art project: try different color combinations, experiment with different cookies, buy five types of multi-color sprinkles and edible glitter—let your creative juices flow!

1½ cups [105 g] Nilla wafers (30 to 35 cookies)

12 oz [340 g] cream cheese, at room temperature

Red, orange, yellow, green, blue, and purple food coloring

½ cup [80 g] rainbow sprinkles or edible glitter

Prep time
50 minutes

1. Pulse the Nilla wafers in a food processor or blender until finely crumbled.

2. Combine the Nilla wafer crumbs and the cream cheese in a bowl. With an electric mixer, beat on medium speed until incorporated. Divide the mixture into 6 equal pieces, one for each color of the rainbow. Place each piece into its own mixing bowl.

3. Add 2 or 3 drops of red, orange, yellow, green, blue, or purple food coloring to each of the six bowls. Stir each mixture individually to make red-, orange-, yellow-, green-, blue-, and purple-colored mixtures.

continued

4. Roll each of the individual mixtures into small balls with the palms of your hands. Once all six have been rolled into small balls, gather them together in one hand and gently press them together, blending and rolling them together to make one large ball. Be careful not to mix the colors too much so they retain their distinctive hues. Form the mixture into a ball and refrigerate until set (see page 8 for instructions).

5. About 30 minutes before serving, remove the cheese ball from the fridge and let it soften at room temperature. Just before serving, spread the rainbow sprinkles onto a rimmed plate. Roll the ball in the rainbow sprinkles, pressing them firmly to the ball, until completely covered. Serve.

Serve with: animal crackers, butter biscuits

Maple Bourbon

This cheese ball employs a lot of classic Southern ingredients, for a dessert that's irresistibly sweet and even a touch naughty. For an alcohol-free version, replace the bourbon with a teaspoon of vanilla extract.

1 cup [70 g] Nilla wafers (approximately 20 cookies)

8 oz [230 g] cream cheese, at room temperature

¼ cup [85 g] maple syrup

1 Tbsp bourbon

6 oz [170 g] toasted pecans (see page 8 for How to Toast Nuts)

**Prep time
1 hour**

1. Pulse the Nilla wafers in a food processor or blender until finely crumbled.

2. Combine the Nilla wafer crumbs, cream cheese, maple syrup, and bourbon in a bowl. With an electric mixer, beat on medium speed until combined. Form the mixture into a ball and refrigerate until set (see page 8 for instructions). Once the cheese ball is set, continue with the instructions for shaping the Hedgehog (see page 12), and then return to the fridge.

continued

3. While the cheese ball sets, coarsely chop the pecans and spread onto a rimmed plate.

4. About 30 minutes before serving, remove the cheese ball from the fridge and let it soften at room temperature. Just before serving, roll the ball in the pecans, pressing them firmly to the ball, until completely covered. Serve.

Serve with: pecan cookies, waffle cookies, molasses cookies

Matcha

This savory tea has moved beyond drinks and makes for a surprising and delectable cheese ball. Serve this alongside a teatime spread or as an eye-catching dessert at the end of a light dinner party.

8 oz [230 g] cream cheese, at room temperature

2 tsp matcha tea powder

¼ cup [70 g] almond paste

¼ cup [30 g] almond meal

1 tsp unsweetened cocoa powder

1 tsp sesame seeds (optional)

**Prep time
40 minutes**

1. Combine the cream cheese, 1 tsp of the matcha, the almond paste, and the almond meal in a bowl. With an electric mixer, beat on medium speed until incorporated. Form the mixture into a ball and refrigerate until set (see page 8 for instructions).

2. About 10 minutes before serving, remove the cheese ball from the fridge and let it soften at room temperature (this ball tends to be softer, so keep it in the fridge until the last moment). Just before serving, stir together the remaining 1 tsp matcha and the cocoa in a small bowl. Using a sifter or a fine-mesh wire strainer, sprinkle the powder mixture over the cheese ball. Scatter the sesame seeds on top, if using. Serve.

Serve with: Nilla wafers, almond cookies, shortbread cookies, sesame crackers

THANKS

First and foremost, this book wouldn't have ever happened if my editors, Deanne and Sarah B., hadn't believed in me from day one—thank you so much for all your encouragement and positivity! Also, a huge thank-you goes out to the whole team at Chronicle Books and the crew at Intern Alley.

My deepest thanks and love to my mom, grandma, and my brother, Omar, for maintaining a constant stream of destressing texts, GIFs, and hugs, and providing much-needed comfort food when all I had in the fridge was cheese. I am forever grateful to my team at the SF SPCA who tirelessly and selflessly taste-tested a bevy of cheese balls—you are the true cheese heroes.

Finally, I'd like to thank, from the bottom of my cheese-encrusted heart, my partner, Zach. Thank you for staying up with me on those late-night recipe testing days, allowing me to come up to you randomly with a smear of cheese ball and demand you taste it, and for being my one-man support system.

I love you!